GREAT AMERICAN
Illustrators

GREAT AMERICAN

ABBEVILLE PRESS • PUBLISHERS

NEW YORK

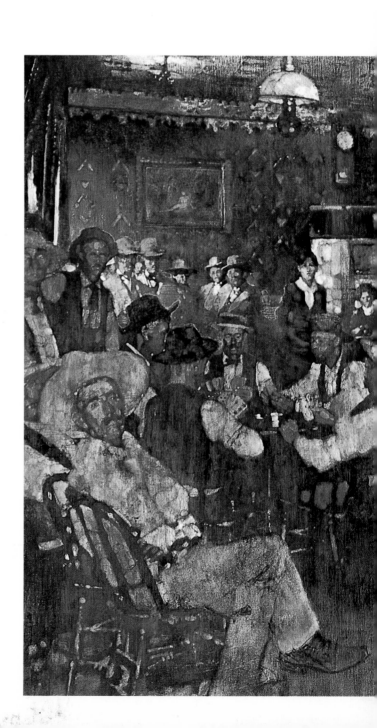

Illustrators

BY WALT REED

ON THE COVER:
Edward Penfield *Young Woman on a Veranda*
Commentary on page 114

ON THE TITLE PAGE:
Bernard Fuchs   *Old Western Saloon*
Courtesy Jack O'Grady Galleries
Commentary on page 70

*Dedicated to all of the other great American
illustrators, past and present, who could not be
included here but who deserve the same recognition.*
W.R.

Library of Congress Catalog Card Number: 79-5378
ISBN: 0-89659-075-5

CONTENTS

INTRODUCTION

Magazine art and museum art have traditionally been worlds apart.

Of the many millions of Americans who have enjoyed pictures in magazines, a comparatively small number regularly go to museum exhibitions.

Early periodicals, such as *Harper's, Scribner's,* and *The Century* were founded to inform and enlighten a developing country. Their editorial content was generally concerned with biography, science, politics, religion, or history. Fiction, in the form of serialized novels or short stories, was gradually added for entertainment.

Sometimes an artist was commissioned to illustrate an incident from one of the articles or stories to relieve the solid pages of type. It was soon found that readers enjoyed the pictures and were more likely to read the material if illustrated. And similarly, readership (and newsstand sales) of a magazine was greatly increased if an illustrated cover was added.

Meanwhile, techniques for reproduction of the art work were improved, progressing from handmade wood engravings to the more accurate, mechanical processes of halftone engraving and finally to color printing.

By the turn of the century magazines were becoming a mass medium with circulation increasing from issue to issue and new publications appearing regularly. The capacity to entertain became a more important factor in competition with other magazines. That entertainment was in the form of fiction, which was produced by some of America's best authors, such as Mark Twain, Booth Tarkington, and F. Scott Fitzgerald. Each story was accompanied by one or more illustrations to convey the nature of the story, set its stage, portray its characters, and present an intriguing incident that would cause the casual page flipper to become a reader.

The artists selected to illustrate the stories or paint the covers were chosen for their popular appeal. The works of artists such as Charles Dana Gibson, Howard Pyle, Maxfield Parrish, Frederic Remington, James Montgomery Flagg, or Norman Rockwell became as well known to readers as the work of the authors.

And, the audience was responsive. Frederic Remington helped to popularize the Old West. Howard Pyle made American history and the chivalry of the Middle Ages come alive again. The Gibson Girl became an ideal for millions of young women—and men. She was followed by a long procession of pretty women: Howard Chandler Christy's Christy Girl, the Coles Phillips Fadeaway Girl, Harrison Fisher's beauties, and Bradshaw Crandell's girls regularly graced the covers of such magazines as *Cosmopolitan, Hearst's International,* the old *Life, Judge, Good Housekeeping, Red Book, Smart Set, College Humor, Woman's Home Companion, Delineator,* and many others. Even the advertising illustrations had their followers; J. C. Leyendecker created an Arrow Collar Man so handsome that he attracted fan mail of his own and even proposals of marriage from smitten young ladies who thought he was real. For many years, Henry Raleigh's aristocratic socialites helped to sell Maxwell House Coffee; N. C. Wyeth advertised Cream of Wheat, and Jessie Willcox Smith advocated the purity of Ivory Soap for mothers with growing children.

Certainly one of the most popular and best-known American illustrators is Norman Rockwell, whose covers for the *Saturday Evening Post* appeared regularly for over fifty years. Rockwell's work reflected perhaps a vanishing reality, but it communicated an enduring vision: an America rooted in the small-town, turn-of-the-century virtues. His work demonstrates the special ability of illustration to capture a moment in time, to record it faithfully, and to have it serve first as mirror, then as memory. The American public's love for Rockwell and the consistent popularity of his illustrations testify to the special relationship that can develop between the illustrator, his magazine, and his public—a relationship unique to this genre.

Because of their great following, the illustrators were well paid, and they influenced popular taste much more than their artist contemporaries who painted only for galleries or museums. As an artist for hire, however, the illustrator has had to work within greater limitations than a gallery artist. Rather than paint only what conviction dictated, he had to carry out the wishes of the client first.

The best illustrators have been able to take these limitations in stride, to make good pictures within the narrow strictures imposed by art editors or advertisers. In conscientiously applying his art to his immediate task and in trying to work within the limitations imposed, however, the illustrator has not usually been concerned about the long-range impact of his work.

Certainly the critics have not been kind to illustrators. It has been fashionable to dismiss illustration as "commercial" art. Yet a review of pictures produced in past decades reveals many of them to be vigorous genre paintings that authentically document their times. Discerning collectors and critics have begun to recognize the artistic merit of these pictures, some of which are now being acquired for museum collections. The gap between museum and magazine art has thereby grown narrower and will undoubtedly continue to do so.

The collection in this book is presented as a small sampling of some of the favorite artists' works. They are not all of equal artistic merit, but each presents an image of its time and provides a vital view of our recent past. While their acceptance as important art must await the verdict of history, they are available here for our present edification and enjoyment.

Walt Reed
Westport, Connecticut

GREAT AMERICAN
Illustrators

"His house was known to all the Vagrant Train"

The Wandering Minstrel

Opposite Page

Illustration for Shakespeare's Henry IV, Part I
Published in Harper's Monthly, 1906
Collection Yale University Art Gallery

Edwin Austin Abbey, N.A., R.A. (1852–1911)

THE EXCELLENCE OF ABBEY'S WORK was a major influence in creating the "Golden Age of American Illustration." Along with A.B. Frost, Howard Pyle, Frederic Remington, E.W. Kemble, Charles Dana Gibson, and Joseph Pennell in the 1880s and 1890s, Abbey helped to make American illustration the finest in the world.

Abbey's devotion to historical accuracy in his pictures led him to England for the original settings and source material for illustrating a book of Robert Herrick's poems. Further assignments to illustrate Shakespeare's plays for *Harper's Magazine* led him to stay in England for most of the rest of his life. Even his monumental murals for the Boston Public Library and for the State Capitol in Harrisburg, Pennsylvania, were painted in England. A large collection of his work is in the permanent collection of the Yale University Art Gallery.

AT LEFT: *Illustration for*
"Froze in August," By Mark Hager
Published in Collier's magazine, 1943

AT RIGHT: *Lonely Lover*
Published in Collier's magazine

BELOW, AT LEFT: *Cartoon of Beckhoff*
by James Montgomery Flagg

BELOW, AT RIGHT: *Typical Beckhoff*
thumbnail sketch, actual size

MR. BECKHOFF BY ENLARGING ONE OF HIS MURALS 700 TIMES AND WITH THE AID OF A PAIR OF POWERFUL MARINE GLASSES, FOR THE FIRST TIME SEES ONE OF HIS FIGURES AND LIKES IT!

FROM HIS FRIEND & ADMIRER JIM FLAGG

Opposite Page

The Turning of the Tables
Pen line and colored inks 15 × 20"
Published in Collier's magazine

Harry Beckhoff (1901–1979)

Many illustrators plan their compositions by means of "thumb-nail" sketches—small and loosely drawn—mainly to establish the placement of the various elements of the picture. Later, a larger, more carefully drawn version would be made prior to the finished painting.

Harry Beckhoff, however, drew his thumb-nails as carefully as the finish, and each is a miniature work of art. Later, these were pantographed to full size. His fellow illustrators marveled at this practice and one of them, James Montgomery Flagg, did the cartoon reproduced here, which spoofed Beckhoff at work.

Beckhoff's drawings are essentially linear, with watercolor washes added, in the tradition of the French illustrators Brissaud, Martin, and Marty, whom he greatly admired. Some of Beckhoff's best illustrations, including a long series of stories by the late Damon Runyon, were made for *Collier's* magazine.

Illustration for "Ommirandy," by Armistead C. Gordon
Published in Scribner's magazine, December, 1914

Illustration for "Peter Ashley," by DuBose Heyward
Published in Woman's Home Companion

Walter Biggs, N.A. (1886–1968)

A SOUTHERNER, BORN IN Elliston, Virginia, Walter Biggs went to New York to study art. He was fortunate to become a student of Robert Henri and to be among an unusually talented group of fellow students, which included Eugene Speicher, Edward Hopper, Rockwell Kent, George Bellows, and Guy Pène Dubois.

Biggs painted both for the gallery and for the magazines. His work is always distinguished by its richness of color and deft control; as he became older, his pictures were increasingly impressionistic. For years he was a mainstay of the *Ladies' Home Journal,* and his work appeared in most of the other magazines.

He was also a teacher at the Art Students League and the Grand Central School of Art—Pruett Carter was among his best-known students. Shortly before his death, **Biggs** was elected to the Hall of Fame of the Society of Illustrators.

Night Sleigh Ride

Illustration published in The Ladies' Home Journal, February, 1917
Copyright © 1917 by the LHJ Publishing Company

Franklin Booth (1874–1948)

THE PICTURES OF Franklin Booth are unmistakable. His pen-and-ink technique was self-taught and was based upon his attempts to duplicate the wood engravings in the books he saw as a farm boy in Indiana. Mistakenly believing them to be pen-and-ink drawings, he laboriously copied them line for line and in the process developed a marvelously controlled and detailed line technique.

In addition to the excellence of his craftsmanship, Booth also had an unusual sense of composition. Although his drawings are actually small in size, they appear to be large in scale with a feeling of great space and height.

Editors found Booth's work to be especially effective in the illustration of poetry or of editorial commentary. He also did striking advertising illustration for such clients as the Esty Organ Company and Zenith Radio.

From "Florian Slappy," by Octavius Roy Cohen
The Saturday Evening Post
© 1938 Curtis Publishing Co.

From "Love's Almost Very,"
by Booth Tarkington
The Saturday Evening Post
© 1934 Curtis Publishing Co.

George Brehm (1878–1966)

GEORGE BREHM WAS A STUDENT of John Twachtman, George Bridgman, Frank Dumond, and Robert Henry, but he found it difficult to get started as an illustrator. He first worked as a newspaper artist for the newly established *Indianapolis Star* in his home state, reporting on politics, trials, and other news events. This led him to illustrate for the *Reader's Magazine* published by Bobbs Merrill in Indianapolis. On the strength of this experience, he moved to New York to try for the major magazines. He began work for *Puck* and *Judge*—humor periodicals—and then with his illustrations for *Delineator* his career was launched. Like his younger brother, Worth, George was at his best with situations involving children and for years illustrated such stories by Booth Tarkington for *The Saturday Evening Post*.

Loafers at the Stable · Woman's Home Companion
Charcoal 17 ¼ × 25 ½" · Collection the author

From "Mumblety-Peg and Middle Age,"
by Walter Prichard Eaton
Scribner's magazine, August, 1911

Opposite Page

From "Tom Sawyer" by Mark Twain
Published by Harper and Brothers, 1910
Charcoal 22 × 14 ¾"

Worth Brehm (1883–1928)

THE YOUNGER BROTHER OF GEORGE BREHM, Worth was inspired by George's interest in art. Both owed much to their small town upbringing in Noblesville, Indiana. In fact, Worth got his start as an illustrator by making a series of charcoal drawings of incidents in the life of a small town boy. He took these drawings to New York and immediately sold them all to *Outing Magazine.* After these pictures were published, *Harper's* asked him to illustrate new editions of *Huckleberry Finn* and *The Adventures of Tom Sawyer.* This assignment led to a long association with *Cosmopolitan Magazine,* illustrating the Penrod stories by Booth Tarkington. He also worked for other magazines and for many other authors, including Sherwood Anderson and Irvin S. Cobb.

WORTH BREHM

The Ultra Intellectual
Reprinted courtesy of Triangle Publ., Inc.

From "The Fast Changing South"
Look magazine, Nov. 16, 1965
© *1965 Cowles Communications*

Austin Briggs (1909–1973)

THE LONG CAREER OF AUSTIN BRIGGS was marked by consistent experimentation and artistic growth. He was a pacesetter whose work was a challenge to other artists.

Briggs grew up in Detroit, Michigan, where he obtained a scholarship to the Wicker Art School. After a short period of study there, he began his art career as an assistant to an automobile illustrator. His job was to put the figures in the pictures. This was followed by drawings for the *Dearborn Independent,* a move to New York for more schooling at the Art Students League, and then any art job he could find during the Depression. He "ghosted" the Flash Gordon comic strip and did pulp illustrations for *Blue Book Magazine.* The magazine work was a valuable training ground, preparing **Briggs** for the opportunity, when it came, to illustrate for most of the major magazines.

The Past Hunters
McCall's magazine, Oct., 1929
Oil 37 × 36" · Collection the author

From "Ye Create Astonishments,"
by Eleanor Hollowell Abbott
Ladies' Home Journal, Dec., 1921
Copyright© 1921 LHJ Publ. Co.

Opposite Page

From the Ladies' Home Journal, Nov., 1927
Copyright© 1927 LHJ Publ. Co.

Pruett Carter (1891–1955)

Few illustrators used color more effectively than Pruett Carter. From Walter Biggs, his teacher, Carter also learned restraint and good taste. There is seldom any violent action in his pictures, and his characterizations are sympathetic—the men modestly handsome, the women well-bred and beautiful. This made him an ideal illustrator for love stories in the women's magazines and he contributed to them for over three decades.

From the first art job on the Hearst *American* in New York and a stint on the *Atlanta Georgian,* he graduated to the art editorship of *Good Housekeeping* magazine. There he assigned manuscripts to be illustrated to other artists, but he also had ambitions to be an illustrator himself. Finally, under Biggs's tutelage he felt ready to try and assigned a story to himself. It was very well received and launched his long and successful career.

A typical "Christy" girl, 1909

"Capture of the Fort"—Spanish American War, 1898

Opposite Page

Illustration for Liberty Bells—Lexington, 1775
Published by the Bobbs-Merrill Company, 1912

Howard Chandler Christy (1873–1952)

Christy's paintings were always large and full of flourish. Everything about his career seemed a little larger than life, including his huge 20 × 30 foot painting, The Signing of the Declaration of Independence, which hangs in the rotunda of the Capitol in Washington, D.C. He also painted portraits of many of the notables of his time, including Secretary of State Charles Evans Hughes, Mrs. Calvin Coolidge, Amelia Earhart, and Mrs. William Randolph Hearst.

His art career began as an artist-reporter accompanying the American troops to Cuba during the Spanish-American War. He did a number of paintings of the action that were published by *Scribner's* and *Leslie's Weekly*. Among his pictures was an imaginary, beautiful girl titled *The Soldier's Dream.* It was well received, and upon his return he began more and more to paint pretty young women; they became known as the "Christy Girls." Christy regularly illustrated magazine stories, drew cover designs, and taught at various art schools. In the latter part of his career he concentrated on mural decorations and society portraits.

Mail Drop from the Sky—Advertising illustration, 1940

Benton Clark (1895–1964)

THE SON OF A HARNESS maker in Coshocton, Ohio, Benton Clark knew horses, wagons, and all the details of harnessing horses. Since he specialized in historic subject matter his knowledge of horses was invaluable.

Clark studied at the Art Institute of Chicago and the National Academy of Design school in New York. He got most of his artistic inspiration, however, from the work of two men, Harvey Dunn for his color and composition, and Frank Hoffman for his black and white dry-brush. Clark himself was a good dramatist. This may have come from his earlier experience in the art department of the Metro Goldwyn Mayer studio in California. His pictures were colorful, convincing, and forceful. For many years Clark's work appeared in *The Saturday Evening Post, Good Housekeeping, McCall's, Cosmopolitan, Blue Book,* and other magazines.

Lydius House, Albany, in 1795

Opposite Page

Circus Capture · Oil on canvas 30½ × 34½"
Published in American magazine, 1934
Collection of the New Britain, Conn., Museum

Matt Clark (1903–1972)

THE BROTHER OF BENTON, and with a similar background, Matt naturally chose the same historical subject matter. In fact, for several years the brothers shared a studio and used the same models, and their work looked very much alike. Matt's painting style was somewhat smoother and more polished, and he perfected a combination of dry-brush and wash or watercolor method that reproduced very effectively. It was also a method that enabled him to work more rapidly than Benton who preferred oils, so Matt was the more prolific. Matt was also more at home with contemporary subject matter, particularly stories involving physical action and high adventure. Matt got his first illustration assignment from *College Humor* magazine. He did a lot of western illustrations for *Collier's* magazine, *The Saturday Evening Post,* and many other magazines.

Something for the Pot
Oil on canvas 24 × 40"

Advertising illustration for the
New England Mutual Life Insurance Co.

John Clymer (born 1907)

J OHN CLYMER WAS BORN IN ELLENSBURG, WASHINGTON. This small town, surrounded by mountains and forests, gave Clymer a lifelong interest in wildlife and nature. He attended the Vancouver School of Art as well as the Ontario College of Art in Canada before returning to the States for training under Frank Schoonover and Harvey Dunn.

Clymer's illustrations first appeared in Canadian magazines, then *Blue Book,* and eventually in most of the major American magazines. For several years he traveled the country painting subjects for *Saturday Evening Post* covers. Meanwhile, he was also painting animal and historical subjects for Grand Central Art Galleries. He now confines himself entirely to paintings of Western history. To research his subjects, Clymer goes to the actual sites of the events in order to observe the terrain and to make landscape studies. He also consults with scholars and museums.

Illustration for a story about Galloping Dick by H.B. Marriott Watson
Published by Associated Sunday Magazines

Illustration for "The White Peacock," by Sax Rohmer
Published in Collier's Weekly magazine, March 6, 1915

Opposite Page

Sir Nigel · Watercolor
Cover illustration for Associated Sunday Magazines

Joseph Clement Coll (1881–1921)

THE REPUTATION OF Coll is primarily based on his pen-and-ink illustrations, although he was a good colorist and a capable painter. His pen-and-ink drawings, however, were a class apart. His idol was the Spanish master, Daniel Vierge, and he successfully emulated Vierge's dazzling variety of pen strokes with the use of solid blacks to obtain a complete range of values and textures. Coupled with this virtuosity was Coll's own remarkable imagination and unique point of view. He was an ideal illustrator for stories by Arthur Conan Doyle, such as "The Lost World" and "Sir Nigel," as well as for the long series of adventures of Fu Manchu by Sax Rohmer in *Collier's Weekly*.

Sir Nigel

A Companion to The White Company

From "Fighting Man," by Quentin Reynolds
Collier's Weekly, Dec. 7, 1935

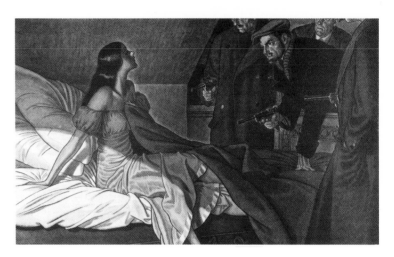

From "Woman of Honor," by James Bellah
Collier's Weekly, June 23, 1934

Opposite Page

From "The Distances of the World," by Michael Foster
Collier's Weekly March 6, 1943
Colored inks 14 ½ × 16 ½" · Collection the artist

Mario Cooper, N.A., A.W.S. (born 1905)

Mario Cooper has worked in all areas of the art field: from sketching and lettering in an advertising agency to magazine illustration and sculpture. He also wrote books on painting and was elected into the National Academy and to the presidency of the American Watercolor Society.

Cooper was born in Mexico City and grew up in Los Angeles where he went to school at the Otis Art Institute and the Chouinard Art Institute. Later he attended Columbia University and the Grand Central School of Art where he studied with Pruett Carter and Harvey Dunn. He himself has taught for many years. His illustrations are distinctive for their dramatic settings and unusual points of view, often seen from above or below the normal eye level. For many years his work was a mainstay of *Collier's Weekly*, but it also appeared in most of the other national magazines.

George Sea Otter from
"The Valley of the Giants," by Peter B. Kyne
Published by *Redbook magazine, November, 1917*

"The City of Jerusalem" from City of the Great King
Published by the Cosmopolitan Book Corporation, 1926

Opposite Page

The Race of the 'Natchez' and the 'Robert E. Lee'
Oil on canvas
Collection, Boatmen's National Bank of St. Louis, Mo.

Dean Cornwell, N.A. (1892–1960)

Duringhisyearsasan illustrator, Dean Cornwell dominated the field. He was an early student of Harvey Dunn, and to Dunn's approach he added his own talent for pictorial organization and composition. His practice was to make dozens of carefully worked-out variations on a picture project with many more supporting drawings of models and sketches of settings. These were followed by another series of color variations. Such thorough preparation made his finished paintings complex but seemingly effortless.

Cornwell later concentrated on mural painting, studying under the British muralist Frank Brangwyn to prepare himself for his first project, a large decoration for the Los Angeles Public Library. This mural, which was done at considerable financial sacrifice, was followed by others, as in the Davidson County Court House, Nashville, Tennessee, the Lincoln Memorial in Redlands, California, and the Eastern Airlines office in New York. Sometimes he would return to magazine illustration to replenish his income, but mural painting remained his greatest interest.

Blazing the Trail Then—And Now
Puck magazine, 1907 · Pen and ink

Opposite Page

Spearing the Water Buffalo
Pen and ink 20½ × 13"
New Britain (Ct.) Museum of American A

Will Crawford (1869–1944)

WILL CRAWFORD BEGAN HIS CAREER as a newspaper artist on the Newark (N.J.) *Call* and early mastered the use of pen and ink. It was always his preferred medium, and his expressive technique, combined with a playful sense of humor, made him a popular contributor to humor magazines, such as *Puck* and the old *Life*. He especially enjoyed concocting elaborate tableaux of improbable historic events—of the past or the future.

Crawford spent some time in Indian territory and was an authority on the American frontier. He was also a good friend of the Western illustrator, Charles Russell, and it is apparent that Russell improved his own pen-and-ink technique through Crawford's example. Among the books Crawford illustrated were *Long Remember* and *Romance of Rosy Ridge* by MacKinlay Kantor, as well as works by Owen Wister.

Illustration for "Tomorrow," by William Faulkner
Published in The Saturday Evening Post
Copyright © 1940 by the Curtis Publishing Company
Collection of the New Britain, Conn., Museum

"London Underground, 1943" from "England at War"
Published by Life magazine, April 3, 1944.

Opposite Page

Illustration for "Last Act, Last Scene," by Alment Jenks
Published in The Saturday Evening Post
Copyright © 1939 by the Curtis Publishing Company
Collection of the New Britain, Conn., Museum

Floyd Davis (1896–1966)

DURING THE EARLY PART OF Floyd Davis's career, he was known for his ability to create high society types, and he was frequently commissioned to do such subjects, especially for advertisers who wanted to confer social status on their products.

Davis's preference, however, was for more down-to-earth subject matter. He particularly enjoyed painting such characters as skid row bums or frowzy scrub-women. His memory was remarkably retentive, and he did not need models in front of him to reconstruct them. When he was assigned a series of hillbilly stories for *The Saturday Evening Post* in the thirties, he was in his element and filled his pictures with unusual characters and special Davis details for the discerning viewer to find.

During World War II, Davis was an artist-war correspondent for *Life* magazine, and his pictures from Britain and other theaters were published by *Life*. These are now part of the National Archives, some displayed in the Pentagon building, Washington, D.C.

Illustration for "The Man Who Understood Women," by Robert Knowlton
Published by Good Housekeeping magazine, August, 1963

Illustration for "Child of the Underworld," by Frank Hanney
Published by Good Housekeeping magazine, August, 1963

Opposite Page

Illustration for "No Visitors 'til Noon"
Published in The Saturday Evening Post
Copyright © 1963 by the Curtis Publishing Company
Collection of the New Britain, Conn., Museum

Joseph DeMers (born 1910)

THE PRETTY GIRL HAS remained one of the most popular illustration subjects even as the public ideal of beauty continues to change. Periodically a new artist comes along who successfully captures that elusive quality. In the 1960s, Joe DeMers was one of the most successful painters of fictional heroines. His types were varied but freely painted and more suggested than meticulously delineated. Guidance from his wife, Janice, helped to insure the appropriateness of their fashions.

DeMers is a Californian. He studied at the Chouinard Art School in Los Angeles where his teachers were Pruett Carter and Lawrence Murphy. Later he studied with Reuben Tam at the Brooklyn Museum Art School. His first employment was as a production designer and illustrator for Hollywood movie studios with a long stay at Warner Brothers. This was followed by illustration assignments for *Fortune* magazine, *Esquire*, and many other national magazines.

46

"Haunted House," advertising illustration for The Barrett Company, 1941

Independence Day
Cover painting reprinted from The Saturday Evening Post, July, 1947
Copyright © 1947 by the Curtis Publishing Company

Opposite Page

Penny Candy · Published in The Saturday Evening Post
Copyright © 1944 by the Curtis Publishing Company
Collection of Sherm Small

Stevan Dohanos (born 1907)

Rᴇsᴇᴀʀᴄʜ ᴘʟᴀʏs ᴀ ʙɪɢ ʀoʟᴇ in the work of Stevan Dohanos. When he takes on an illustration assignment, he wants to know everything possible about the subject. This involves maps, examples of all the costumes or props that will be in the picture, and interviews with experts in the field if the subject is new to him. Then he is ready to consider the artistic problems of composing and rendering the picture. Such meticulous attention to detail helped to make him so popular as a cover artist for *The Saturday Evening Post* where readers would scrutinize each new cover for any possible errors.

In his long career, Dohanos has illustrated for most of the magazines and executed several Federal mural commissions; his paintings are in many public and private collections. He has designed twenty-five U.S. postage stamps, and for many years he has been a member of the Citizens Advisory Committee of the U.S. Postal Service.

Albert Dorne (1904–1965)

ONE OF THE HALLMARKS of the skill of an artist is demonstrated in the ability to draw heads and hands. Al Dorne prided himself on being a "pro" and he made expressive use of facial characterizations and poses of hands in every conceivable position. Dorne was especially effective with New York characters. Born and brought up on the Lower East

Side of New York City, he left school in the eighth grade to help support his family. He got his artistic start as an assistant to illustrator Saul Tepper and eventually went on to do freelance advertising and editorial illustration for all of the major magazines.

Dorne became president of the Society of Illustrators and was a co-founder of the Code of Ethics and Fair Practices of the Profession of Commercial Art and Illustration. In 1948 he founded and directed the Famous Artists School with a distinguished faculty of outstanding illustrators. He was the recipient of many honors, including the Horatio Alger Award for Achievement from the American Schools and Colleges Association.

World War I reportorial drawing of troops crossing a river

Shingling the Roof, 1916

Opposite Page

Buffalo Bones Plowed Under
Oil on canvas 24 × 40"
Collection of Harold Von Schmidt

Harvey Dunn, N.A. (1884–1952)

THE SON OF A HOMESTEADING pioneer in South Dakota, Harvey Dunn was brought up on hard work. To pay for his schooling at the Art Institute of Chicago, he worked for his neighbor farmers, plowing up the virgin sod of "buffalo grass"—he developed a powerful physique in the process.

Following his studies at the Institute, he was accepted by master illustrator Howard Pyle for further training in Wilmington, Delaware. Dunn's illustration career was interrupted by World War I when he and seven other leading illustrators were commissioned as captains in the A.E.F. with orders to the front to record the lives and action of the men in documentary drawings and paintings. Dunn's pictures, based on shared dangers in the trenches and "over the top" are among the best of an important war collection in the Smithsonian Institution in Washington. Some of Dunn's finest paintings are in the collection at the South Dakota Memorial Art Center in Brookings.

Little Women · Reader's Digest, 1965

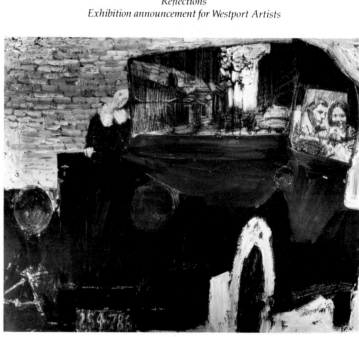

Reflections
Exhibition announcement for Westport Artists

Opposite Page

Portrait of George Rogers Clark
For the National Park Service, 1975
Acrylic 48 × 36" · Collection the artist

Mark English (born 1933)

Reflecting the many changes which have occurred in the field of illustration in the last decade, the work of Mark English has also undergone great changes. In the process he has been in the vanguard, setting the pace for many of his contemporaries.

English was born in Texas and went to the university there. He then studied at the Art Center School in Los Angeles where John LaGatta was one of his instructors. His first studio experience was in Detroit for the automobile industry, providing figures and settings for display of the cars. His first fiction illustration was for *The Saturday Evening Post*, and he has worked for most of the other magazines since. During this time his work has become progressively less literal, more stylized and decorative. He is particularly effective in a montage approach in which more than one idea or event may be combined in a single painting.

Carl Oscar August Erickson (1891–1958)

HIS ELEGANT FASHION DRAWINGS signed simply "Eric" were immediately recognizable as the work of a master. Both in his knowledge of fashion and in the quality of his watercolor paintings and drawings, Erickson was the most famous fashion artist in Paris and in America for decades.

Erickson was from Illinois, and he studied at the Chicago Academy of Fine Arts. He first worked for Marshall Field and other advertising clients before moving to New York and beginning his fashion career, drawing for the *Dry Goods Economist.* Eventually, he went to Paris and joined the art staff of *Vogue* magazine there. After twenty years he returned to the United States, continuing his association with *Vogue*, regularly reporting on Paris openings and producing volumes of illustrations and many cover paintings. A fashion plate himself, he carried a walking stick, wore a bowler hat, and always had a fresh flower in his lapel.

V-Mail · Published in The Saturday Evening Post
Copyright © 1943 by the Curtis Publishing Company

East Meets West—Promontory Point, Utah, May 10, 1869
Commissioned by the 3M Company in 1976 as part of a series of paintings
for the Bicentennial · Copyright © 1976 by the 3M Company

Opposite Page

Boys and Kites · Published in The Saturday Evening Post
Copyright © by the Curtis Publishing Company
Collection of the New Britain, Conn., Museum

John Falter (born 1910)

As part of the Bicentennial salute, the 3M Company commissioned John Falter to create a series of six paintings of historical highlights. He was concerned with making them as historically accurate as possible, but in order to prevent a future art historian from misjudging the date of the paintings, he carefully painted modern objects and placed them unobtrusively in each picture. The average viewer, for instance, might not notice or recognize the tear-off tabs of Polaroid film at the feet of the photographer.

Falter was born in Nebraska, studied at the Kansas City Art Institute, and then attended the Art Students League and the Grand Central School of Art in New York. His career began early with illustrating for the "pulps." By the age of twenty, he had graduated to *Liberty* and the rest of the major magazines soon followed. His best-known work was done for the covers of *The Saturday Evening Post,* and his regional subject matter established a whole new direction for *Post* cover art.

Illustration for
"If the South had Won the Civil War,"
by MacKinlay Kantor
Copyright © 1960
by Cowles Communications, Inc.

Illustration for "Young Hickory"
Copyright © 1940 by Stanley Young

Opposite Page

Illustration for "The Adventure of the Black Baronet,"
by Adrian Conan Doyle and John Dickson Carr, 1953
Reprinted from Collier's magazine, 1953

Robert Fawcett (1903–1967)

DURING HIS CAREER, Robert Fawcett was known as the "illustrator's illustrator," greatly admired and respected for the excellence of his pictorial compositions and for his extraordinary draftsmanship.

Fawcett was born in England, migrated with his family to Canada, and returned to England to study art at the well-known Slade School of London University. His drawing skill was developed there and led, many years later, to his book, *On the Art of Drawing*.

On his return from England, he headed for New York where his work began to appear regularly for advertising as well as editorial illustrations. He was able to convincingly depict a wide range of subject matter but was at his very best with a series of illustrations for Sherlock Holmes stories that appeared in *Collier's* magazine in the 1950s. He also created an outstanding group of illustrations for MacKinlay Kantor's provocative article in *Look* magazine, "If the South had Won the Civil War."

Illustration for "Tugboat Annie," by Norman Reilly Raine
Copyright © 1934 by the Curtis Publishing Company

Convoy Escort—advertising illustration for the Sperry Gyroscope Company, 1943

Opposite Page

The Gwydyr Castle
Oil on canvas 28 × 29"
Collection of Les Mansfield

Anton Otto Fischer (1882–1962)

An orphan boy in Germany, Fisher ran away to sea at the age of sixteen. He served his apprenticeship on several sailing ships over the next eight years. Deciding to apply for American citizenship, he stayed in the New York area to work as a hand on racing yachts and taught seamanship on the school ship "St. Mary's." A chance job as a model and handyman for illustrator A. B. Frost introduced him to the world of art, and he decided to follow an illustrator's career. Saving his money, he enrolled in the Académie Julien in Paris where he received sound academic training. Upon his return to the States, he painted a sample picture based on his sailing experience and promptly received an assignment from *Harper's Weekly*. From then on he was in continuous demand from almost every magazine with a manuscript about the sea. His longest association was with *The Saturday Evening Post* for which he illustrated "Tugboat Annie" stories by Norman Reilly Raines and many other series.

Typical "Fisher" girl, illustration for Cosmopolitan magazine, June, 1923

Cosmopolitan magazine cover, May 1934

Opposite Page

*Illustration in The Harrison Fisher Book
Published by Charles Scribner's Sons, 1907
Collection of Mr. and Mrs. Alan Goffman*

Harrison Fisher (1875–1934)

RECEIVING MUCH OF HIS art education in the studio of his father, a landscape painter, Fisher completed his training at the Mark Hopkins Institute of Art in San Francisco. By the age of sixteen his work began to be published in the local San Francisco newspapers. Having been born in the borough of Brooklyn, he decided to return to New York City, where he began to work for *Puck* magazine as a staff artist.

He soon concentrated on pictures of beautiful women, in the manner of Charles Dana Gibson and Howard Chandler Christy. He preferred to work in pastel, a difficult medium but one which reproduced effectively. For many years, to the end of his career, he was under exclusive contract to do the monthly covers—always a pretty girl—for *Cosmopolitan* magazine, and he was also much sought after for private portraiture.

Smoke Dreams, A Bachelor's Reverie

Caricature of George Bernard Shaw
Published in Hearst's International magazine

Opposite Page

Illustration for the American Red Cross, World War I
Watercolor

James Montgomery Flagg (1877–1960)

Probably the single best-known and most reproduced of Flagg's pictures was his famous "I Want *You*" for the U. S. Army recruiting poster showing Uncle Sam pointing directly at the viewer. Printed in the millions, it was used during both world wars.

However, Flagg was a versatile artist, as much a celebrity as the famous people whose portraits he drew or whom he caricatured. Every one he depicted, from presidents to movie stars, were all flattered to pose for this incisive artist. An early effort, a comic strip character, "Nervy Nat," revealed Flagg's tart sense of humor, and he could occasionally lampoon the mighty with devastating effect.

Most of Flagg's career, however, was devoted to fiction illustration; he was a favorite of William Randolph Hearst, who saw to it that Flagg appeared regularly in his magazines. Flagg's preferred medium was pen and ink, but he also worked effectively in watercolor and liked best doing humorous subjects by authors such as P. G. Wodehouse for whom he illustrated many of the "Jeeves" short stories in *Collier's* magazine.

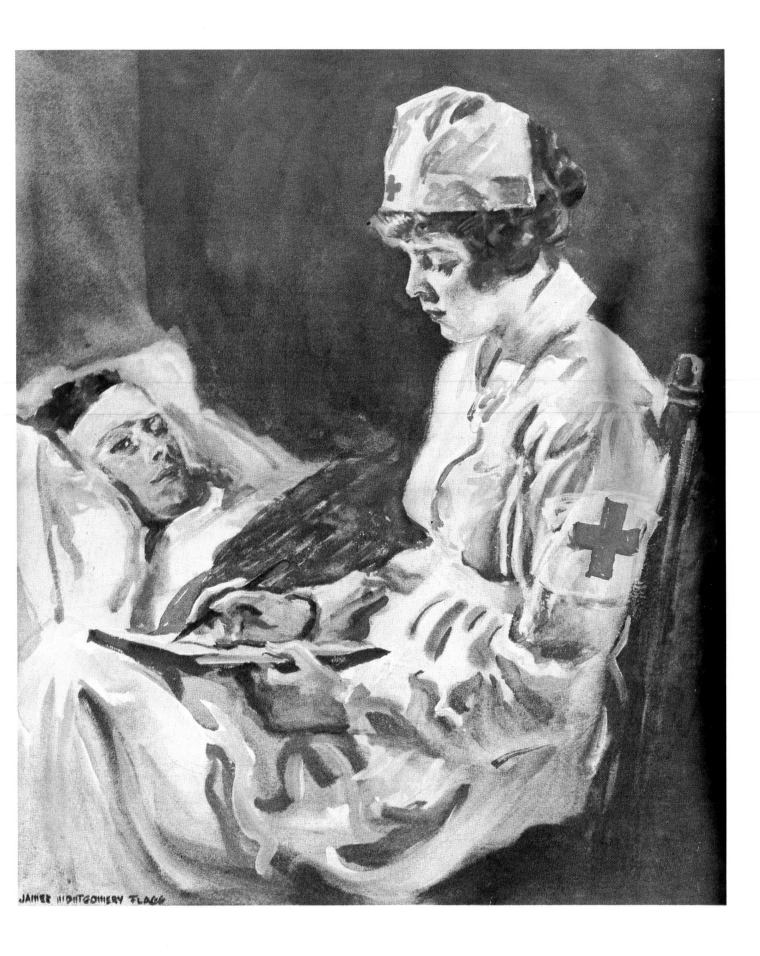

Illustration for Impty-Umpty and the Blacksmith, by Joel Chandler Harris
The Metropolitan magazine

The Itinerant Fiddler

Opposite Page

Grouse Hunting
Reprinted from Scribner's magazine, November, 1916
Collection of Henry M. Reed

Arthur Burdett Frost (1851–1928)

THE WORK OF FROST is probably most closely associated with that of Joel Chandler Harris who wrote the Uncle Remus stories. Harris felt that Frost had an equal share in making his creations come alive through his pictorial interpretations of "Br'er Rabbit" and the rest of the characters.

Frost also revealed his sense of humor in his characterizations of rural folk. In situations such as a checker game in a country store or a political argument in a post office, he faithfully and sympathetically records the manners, dress, and settings of country life in the 1880s and 90s. Frost was also an ardent sportsman. His pictures of hunting and dogs are much prized by collectors today, as are his pictures of golfing subjects. His art career had been launched by his first commissioned work to illustrate a book, *Out of the Hurly Burly.* Both the book and Frost's nearly four hundred illustrations were an instant success, selling over a million copies and leading to work for *Harper's* magazine and a long prolific career.

One of a series of paintings for
Sports Illustrated of the Longchamps race in Paris, not published

Illustration for "U.S. Open Preview"
Published in Sports Illustrated magazine, June 15, 1964
Copyright © 1964 by Time, Inc., Art Director: Richard Gangel

Opposite Page

Illustration for "Portrait of the Artist," by Eileen Jensen
Reprinted from McCall's magazine, July, 1964

Bernard Fuchs (born 1932)

ONE OF THE TOP contemporary illustrators, Fuchs was named "Artist of the Year" in 1962 when he was only thirty. Fuchs is from Illinois and studied at the Washington University Art School in St. Louis. His first art jobs were in Detroit working in studios with automobile accounts. A competitive field with high standards, it proved an excellent training ground for magazine illustration.

After five years he came to New York and began work for most of the magazines and many national advertisers. Over the years Fuchs has been most closely associated with *Sports Illustrated* magazine, which has sent him on assignment as an artist-reporter to cover many national and international sporting events. And, like many other present illustrators, he also pursues an active painting career with many one-man shows.

Gifford Pinchot
Reprinted courtesy of
Weyerhaeuser Timber Co.

Mother Fox and Kids
Reprinted courtesy of
Weyerhaeuser Timber Co.

Opposite Page

Egrets at Home
Reader's Digest cover, Feb., 1978
Watercolor 20 × 16"

Stanley Galli (born 1912)

GALLI FINISHED HIGH SCHOOL DURING THE GREAT DEPRESSION and there was no money for further schooling. So he spent the next several years working at any kind of job he could find: as a ranch hand in Nevada, an apprentice baker in Reno, and as a longshoreman in San Francisco. Eventually, he saved up enough money to attend the San Francisco Institute of Art.

His first art job was for an art service and by the time of World War II, he was a partner in the firm. During the war he was in special service in the navy, working with training methods and materials. He returned to the art service after the war, but he was no longer interested in its time-consuming business aspects, which kept him away from the easel. Embarking upon a freelance illustration career was a big step, but Galli was soon busy on both coasts, illustrating for *The Saturday Evening Post, True, McCall's,* and others.

Nude at a Mirror
Published by Cosmopolitan magazine, January, 1946

Illustration for "The Smoky Years," by Alan Le May
Published in Collier's magazine, January 26, 1935
Collection of the New York Society of Illustrators

Opposite Page

Illustration for Pacific Mills, 1949
Watercolor 21 × 18"
Collection of the author

John Gannam, A.N.A. (1907–1965)

JOHN GANNAM WAS A MASTER watercolorist, the result of a lifelong preoccupation with this challenging medium. He was also the despair of his art editors. Never satisfied with his pictures, he would do them over and over, until the magazine deadlines had long passed. The results were beautiful, however, and worth the wait; his finished pictures looked effortless.

Gannam grew up in Chicago. When he was fourteen, his father died, and he was forced to leave school to work. Eventually he became a messenger for an engraving house and was introduced to the world of art. He began a program of self-education that continued for the rest of his life, long after he had become one of the major illustrators and had won top honors in art directors exhibitions. Among his most memorable pictures were his advertising illustrations for Pacific Mills and St. Mary's Blankets.

Edwin Georgi (1896–1964)

THE ILLUSTRATION CAREER OF EDWIN GEORGI is most closely associated with the beauty of the women he depicted. In his careful, meticulous technique and brilliant use of color, he modeled them with loving detail. For many years his pictures were in most of the major women's magazines.

Georgi had planned to be a civil engineer and was a student at Princeton at the outbreak of World War I. He enlisted in the U. S. Air Force and became a pilot. At loose ends after the war, he found a pasteup job in an advertising agency and decided he wanted to make art his career. Through the agency training, he began to do increasingly important advertising drawings, eventually illustrating for major accounts, such as the Hartford Fire Insurance Company, Hockanum Woolens, and the Crane Paper Company. It was his ability to do fashionable and beautiful women that led to his successful transition to editorial illustration for the magazines.

The Last Guest
Published in Life magazine, 1895

Her Reply, 1914
Collection of Morris Weiss

The Greatest Game in the World—His Move
Published in Collier's Weekly, 1903

Charles Dana Gibson (1867–1944)

Everyone knew who the Gibson Girl was. She was the creation of Charles Dana Gibson, and he was almost as famous as she. At the turn of the century every girl wanted to look like her. She was sung about and portrayed on the stage; her likenesses were painted on plates and printed on pillows and banners. Gibson did not restrict himself to drawing beautiful women, however. Although mostly remembered for his pictures of high society, he effectively delineated characters of all kinds, and many of his drawings record the foibles and problems of people of all classes.

After World War I when the old *Life* magazine was having financial difficulties, Gibson stepped in as owner and editor to revive it through his own drawings and to encourage new talent to contribute. He was successful until the onset of the Depression, which marked the end of *Life* and many other magazines. Gibson retired to paint portraits in oil in the same vigorous manner in which he had earlier used the pen.

Curtain Fire
Collection of F. R. Gruger, Jr.

Illustration for
"Freedom's a Hard Bought Thing,"
by Stephen Vincent Benet ·
Published in The Saturday Evening Post
Copyright © 1940
by the Curtis Publishing Company

Opposite Page

True Thomas—The Last Supper in Modern Dress
Reprinted from Cosmopolitan magazine, August, 1925
Collection of F.R. Gruger, Jr.

Frederic Rodrigo Gruger (1871–1953)

Frederic Gruger, better known as "F.R." Gruger, attended the Pennsylvania Academy of the Fine Arts where he was the schoolmate of future members of "The Eight": John Sloan, William Glackens, and Everett Shinn. And, like them, he first worked as a newspaper artist for various Philadelphia and New York newspapers. This was excellent training for a future illustrator since it was necessary to draw quickly and accurately, and to retain memory of all the details that needed to be added later in making the finished drawing for publication. In fact, Gruger became so adept at figure drawing that he never needed models later in his career.

He was invited by the newly revived *Saturday Evening Post* in 1898 to make some of his first illustrations, and he continued his loyal association with the publication for the next forty years. Gruger's drawings, usually in black-and-white Wolff pencil and wash, are small but look large in print. It is the scale of his compositions that give them a monumental look, and he was a master in relating figures and settings.

TOP: *1908 French Grand Prix*
Published by True magazine, 1953

Telescope—Big Eye
Published in American magazine

Steel Mill Interior
Advertising illustration, 1944

Opposite Page

Illustration for Caterpillar Tractor Company, 1945
Tempera 30 × 30"
Collection of Louis Neumiller

Peter Helck, N.A. (born 1893)

PETER HELCK HAS BEEN IN love with auto racing for almost his whole life. He saw the Vanderbilt Cup Race on Long Island in 1906 and from then on has followed everything having to do with auto racing in America and various parts of the world. In the process, he has become an authority and the foremost painter of the history of racing, documenting many of the outstanding events in two books, *The Checkered Flag*, **published by** Scribner's in 1961, and *The Vanderbilt Cup Races*, published by Harry N. Abrams, Inc. in 1975 for which he was both author and illustrator. His interests also included locomotives, particularly the earlier steam variety, and, as a painter of industrial subjects, he often includes an engine or cars somewhere in the background of his illustrations.

In 1920 Helck was able to meet and study under the noted English muralist, Frank Brangwyn. Ever since, Helck has followed Brangwyn's advice to paint from nature, and he prefers to draw or paint on location rather than rely on photos for information. It has also led to his lifelong practice of painting landscapes, particularly the hilly, picturesque area of upper New York State where he has lived for the last fifty years.

Civilization's Progress—A Happy New Year, "The Days Beyond Recall"

The Happy New Year Today—and the Party Raided
Reproduced by Liberty magazine, January 2, 1932

Opposite Page

Sitting Pretty
Life magazine cover, March 31, 1927
Collection of Mrs. John Held, Jr.

John Held, Jr. (1889–1958)

No ARTIST WAS MORE POPULAR in the 1920s, and no one ever better documented the Jazz Age. His brittle pen line recorded the short-skirted flappers, their sheiks with bell-bottomed trousers, the speakeasies, bathtub gin, necking in the rumble seat, and the rest of the post-World War I youth rebellion. It was a period of great prosperity, and Held was riding high along with it; he had so much work that he could name his own price. He moved to an estate in the country, played polo with his own string of horses, and married a succession of wives.

Held had a second, equally popular art technique—the cutting and printing of wood or linoleum blocks in the manner of the old crude wood engravings, using parodies of Victorian morality for his subjects. Many of these appeared in *The New Yorker* magazine, edited by Harold Ross, his boyhood friend from Salt Lake City. He was also a popular contributor to *College Humor, Cosmopolitan, Liberty* magazine, the old *Life, Judge,* and *Harper's Bazaar.* Held was also a serious watercolorist and sculptor and the author of several books. His biography, *The Most of John Held, Jr.,* was published by Stephen Greene Press in 1972.

March 31 1927
Life
Price 15 cents
John Held Jr.
SITTING PRETTY

The Creators · Published in Century magazine

Illustration for "Her Letter," by Bret Harte

Gallant Rescuer

Opposite Page

Illustration for "Her Letter," by Bret Harte
Published by Houghton, Mifflin and Company, 1905
Collection of the author

Arthur I. Keller (1866–1925)

IN THE NINETEENTH CENTURY most artists looked to Europe for their advanced training. American art schools could not compare with the academic prestige of such schools as the Académie Julien of Paris or the institutes in Munich or Berlin.

Arthur I. Keller was of German descent, and it was natural for him to follow his studies at the National Academy of Design in New York with three years at the Munich Academy. With this excellent background, he had no difficulty in establishing himself as an illustrator when he returned to the U.S. In fact, it is the high artistic calibre of Keller that shines through every example of his work. His figures, always drawn from the model, were painted with charming facility and ease, always convincing in attitude and expression. He was a favorite with editors and the public alike and was given manuscripts by top authors such as Bret Harte, Owen Wister, and Washington Irving. Some of Keller's finest illustrations were done for an edition of Irving's *Legend of Sleepy Hollow*. A collection of his pictures is in the Cabinet of Illustration in the Library of Congress and at the New Britain (Connecticut) Museum of American Art.

There ain't no Excuse for a Woman not Havin' a Good Figger

Three Negroes in Church
Collection of Mrs. Thomas Wilcox

Drawing for Christmas Card, 1886

Opposite Page

Play Ball · Pen and ink drawing
Collier's magazine cover

Edward Windsor Kemble (1861–1933)

Before halftone photoengraving made possible the reproduction of toned drawings that were faithful to the artist's work, pen and ink was the preferred artists' medium. Kemble taught himself to use the pen very effectively.

Since he was of a humorous bent, Kemble was an ideal candidate to illustrate the first edition of Mark Twain's *Huckleberry Finn* and *Puddin' Head Wilson.* He also illustrated many of the stories of *Uncle Remus* by Joel Chandler Harris. He also did many pictures of negro subjects, including Harriet Beecher Stowe's *Uncle Tom's Cabin.* Kemble was occasionally a political cartoonist, and his humor, combined with exaggerated drawings, made him an effective satirist. This same ability also made him an especially good sports reporter.

Collier's

THE NATIONAL WEEKLY

A dive for a base.

A home run

Three strikes and out.

A slide to first

"Oh kill the umpire Please"

The Umpire calls a favorite out.

Some fancy plays

Kemble

"PLAY BALL!"

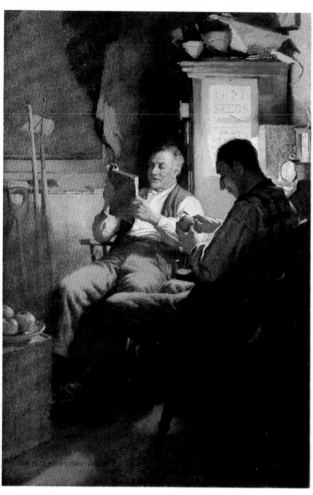

The Spite Fence · Published by Harper's magazine, July, 1913

The Prospector · Cover from The Saturday Evening Post
Copyright © 1933 by the Curtis Publishing Company

Opposite Page

Illustration for "Ranchero Mantanza," by Steward Edward White
Published in The Saturday Evening Post
Copyright © 1931 by the Curtis Publishing Company
Collection of Ruth Koerner Oliver

William Henry Dethlef Koerner (1878–1938)

KOERNER LANDED HIS FIRST JOB when he was only fifteen as a newspaper artist on the *Chicago Tribune*. He learned enough of the rudiments to go on, successively, to a small midwest magazine as an assistant art editor and to freelance in New York. However, he was ambitious to become an illustrator, and he realized that his art training was too limited. Because Howard Pyle was his favorite illustrator, Koerner applied to study at the Pyle School in Wilmington, Delaware. By this time, however, Pyle was no longer conducting the school, but he gave Koerner some special help, as did a number of Pyle's students including Frank Schoonover, Stanley Arthurs, and N. C. Wyeth.

Koerner was a westerner—from Iowa—and he liked best doing illustrations for stories of the Old West. Although at the beginning he was given manuscript subjects ranging from Maine to Africa, he soon became known for his expertise at drawing cowpunchers and horses and eventually was able to specialize in Western subjects. For many years his illustrations appeared regularly in *The Saturday Evening Post*.

Stroud Farm · Oil on masonite 24¾ × 32¼"
Collection Frame House Gallery,
Louisville, Kentucky

Haida Indians Arrive for a Potlatch
Oil on canvas 28 × 40"
Collection Hammer Galleries, N.Y.C.

Opposite Page

Reading the Declaration of Independence: July 9, 1776
Calendar and print for American Cyanamid Co.
Oil on canvas 28 × 38" · Coll. American Cyanamid Co.

Mort Künstler (born 1931)

Mort Künstler's illustrations are almost an anachronism. Although very much a contemporary and productive artist, his artistic leanings—and heroes—are of an earlier era. His thoroughgoing craftsmanship, too, is of the old school. Research plays a large part in Künstler's work, and he may go anywhere in the country to find a particular prop needed to make his pictures authentic or an expert to help him find the right information. He has had many assignments from the *National Geographic,* and he has created series of historical illustrations for such clients as the American Cyanamid Company and the New York Bank for Savings. Künstler also has an active painting and print-making career. He is affiliated with the Hammer Galleries and the Circle Galleries in New York and the Frame House Galley in Louisville, Kentucky. His book *Fifty Epic Paintings of America* was recently published by the Abbeville Press.

Illustration for "The Afterthoughts of Lady Godiva," by John Erskine
Published in Cosmopolitan magazine

Fashion drawing for the William Hengerer Company

Opposite Page

Couple on Balcony
Cosmopolitan magazine, August, 1949
Collection of the New York Society of Illustrators

John LaGatta (1894–1977)

Many artists have specialized in painting the faces of pretty girls. But John LaGatta drew the whole female figure. Although he occasionally did a nude figure, such as Lady Godiva, this was seldom permitted in a family magazine. That was no handicap to LaGatta. Even though his female characters were fully clothed, their gowns only served to accentuate the figure beneath.

Born in Naples, Italy, LaGatta came to the U.S. at an early age and studied at the New York School of Fine and Applied Art under Frank Alvah Parsons and Kenneth Hayes Miller. He began as a fashion illustrator, much under the influence of the French artist Drian. Because he knew style and how to flatter women artistically, his work appeared frequently in all the women's magazines. During the 1930s, LaGatta was one of the most prolific—and highest paid—illustrators. Later he taught illustration at the Art Center School in Los Angeles.

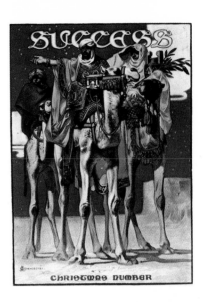

*Cover illustration from The Saturday Evening Post, 1919
Copyright © 1919 by the Curtis Publishing Company*

*Cover illustration from The Saturday Evening Post, 1922
Copyright © 1922 by the Curtis Publishing Company*

Joseph Christian Leyendecker (1874–1951)

For over forty years Leyendecker's paintings decorated the covers of *The Saturday Evening Post,* beginning in 1899; he drew over three hundred subjects for the *Post.* A recurring favorite each year was the New Year's baby with a topical commentary on the times. (As a young man, Norman Rockwell was in great awe of Leyendecker and learned much about cover design from his example.)

One of Leyendecker's most popular creations was the handsome, clean-cut young man he created for the Arrow Collar Company. Although designed to sell collars to the men, each illustration brought fan mail from young women with matrimony in mind.

Leyendecker was born in Germany and came to America at an early age with his brother Frank. After they had attended evening classes at the Chicago Art Institute, the two brothers went to Paris to study at the Académie Julien. They were outstanding students, and returned to the U.S. and to immensely successful careers. Frank died early, at age forty-seven; J.C.'s career continued for many more years.

Collier's
THE NATIONAL WEEKLY

JAMESTOWN 1607

Youth Against Age · Published in Collier's magazine

"Contemplation," illustration for Woman's Home Companion

Opposite Page

*Illustration for "America's One-Man Air Force,"
by Scott Hart and Joseph Millard
Published in True magazine*

Tom Lovell (born 1909)

ONE OF THE TOP PAINTERS of the Old West, Tom Lovell has reached that position through talent and hard work. He has always been a compulsive researcher, and he immerses himself thoroughly in a subject before attempting its interpretation. Small pastel sketches suggest action and color. They are followed by figure studies and finally by a full-scale charcoal rendering to determine placement and black-and-white values. The finished painting is usually in oil.

Lovell studied at Syracuse University, earning a Bachelor of Fine Arts degree. While still in school, he began illustrating for the pulp magazines, both in black and white and in color for covers. Soon his work began to appear in the "slicks," or major magazines, such as *Woman's Home Companion, Cosmopolitan,* and *Collier's.* His abilities for historical research were soon recognized, and for a long time he specialized in pictures for period stories, leading to his present concentration on the Old West.

AT LEFT:
From "The Outlaw of Las Uvas,"
by Bennett Foster
Watercolor · Saturday Evening Post
© 1950 Curtis Publishing Co.

ABOVE RIGHT:
Saturday Evening Post cover, July 21, 1945
Copyright© 1945 Curtis Publ. Co.
Designers colors · Collection the artist

ABOVE LEFT:
From "Coroner Creek," by Luke Short
The Saturday Evening Post, 1945
Watercolor © 1945 Curtis Publ. Co.

Opposite Page

True magazine cover
Opaque watercolor 25 × 19"
Collection the author

Fred Ludekens (born 1900)

FRED LUDEKENS SAT IN A NIGHT ART CLASS CONDUCTED BY OTIS SHEPARD at the University of California Extension in San Francisco, but because he had never had any prior art training, he was too embarrassed to participate. Finally, for the class assignment—a project to be done at home—Ludekens brought in a poster design so good that Shepard promptly offered the young man a job at Foster & Kleiser where he was art director. For many years Ludekens concentrated on advertising clients; his illustrations for a book by a friend, titled *Ghost Town*, attracted the attention of *The Saturday Evening Post* and led to his involvement with editorial illustration. Because of his versatility Ludekens has had a wide variety of assignments, but he particularly enjoys the stories of hunting, animals, and the Old West.

From "Lost Sister," by Dorothy M. Johnson
Collier's magazine

From "The Darkest Hour,"
by William P. McGivern
Collier's magazine, April 29, 1955

Opposite Page

Distant Thunder
Oil 24 × 36"
Collection U.S. Cavalry Museum, Ft. Riley (Kan.)
Copyright © 1976 Frank McCarthy

Frank McCarthy (born 1924)

FRANK McCARTHY DRAWS A SHARP LINE between his earlier work as an illustrator for the magazines and his present career as a painter of the Old West. The absence of deadlines and the opportunity to travel to actual locations to record settings for paintings of his own choosing have made a great difference in the quality of his work. Today, he is one of the most sought after and successful contemporary painters of Western history.

McCarthy studied at Pratt Institute and the Art Students League in New York. Among his teachers were George Bridgman and Reginald Marsh. His magazine illustrations generally dealt with adventure and action, providing the opportunity to do dramatic, arresting pictures. This quality in his work was also appropriate for motion picture posters and for paperback book cover art, and McCarthy had a very successful career in these areas before making the artistic move west.

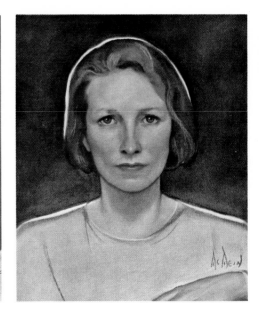

TOP ROW · **reading left to right**

Edna St. Vincent Millay
McCall's magazine cover, July, 1937

Amelia Earhart
McCall's magazine cover, May, 1937

Helen Hayes
McCall's magazine cover, Sept, 1937

AT LEFT
Dorothy Thompson
McCall's magazine cover, Aug, 1937

Opposite Page

The Artist · Pastel
McCall's magazine cover, June 1932

Neysa McMein (1890–1949)

Neysa McMein's studio in New York was as much a gathering place for celebrities as space for her to work in. Alexander Woollcott, George Abbott, Irving Berlin, Marc Connolly, Jascha Heifetz, Dorothy Parker, and many others were her friends, and she had a continuous stream of visitors who might entertain each other while she worked from a model.

Her forte was portraiture. For years she drew pretty girls' faces for *McCall's*, and her work also appeared on covers of *The Saturday Evening Post, Woman's Home Companion*, and other magazines as well as in advertising illustrations. Eventually she abandoned magazine work to do portraiture exclusively and painted many of the outstanding American women of her time. A memorial fund for the purchase of works by living artists has been established in her name by the Whitney Museum of American Art.

Wallace Morgan, N.A. (1873–1948)

WALLACE MORGAN, LIKE MANY ILLUSTRATORS OF HIS ERA, was first a newspaper artist. It was a hectic life, requiring the ability to size up the pictorial possiblities in a situation, make rough on-the-spot sketches, and then translate the notes into finished pen-and-ink drawings in time to meet the deadlines. The ability to draw the figure was a prerequisite. Morgan was so thoroughly trained that he never needed models for his illustrations when he made the transition to magazines. This training also served him well during his assignment in World War I to document the fighting at the front.

Morgan's natural inclination was to humor. He was the ideal illustrator for the P.G. Wodehouse stories in *The Saturday Evening Post,* and his work also appeared regularly in *The New Yorker, Collier's, Woman's Home Companion,* and other magazines.

15. It had the irresponsibility of a cyclone

Illustration for the Ladies' Home Journal,
Copyright © 1948 by LHJ Publishing, Inc.

Mother and Daughter cover for the Ladies' Home Journal
Copyright © 1939 by LHJ Publishing, Inc.

Opposite Page

House Without Doors · Published in Ladies' Home Journal
Copyright © 1954 by the LHJ Publishing Company
Collection of the author

Al Parker (born 1906)

AL PARKER'S ILLUSTRATIONS dominated the magazines for over twenty years, along with those of his imitators who tried to emulate the Parker touch. Characterized by a great diversity and experimentation in many approaches and mediums, however, his work was difficult to copy and his imitators were left behind. Among his innovations was the extreme closeup, the "candid" unposed look of his models, the use of unusual props, and a picture idea strong enough to serve as a "stopper" for the casual magazine reader.

Parker was born in St. Louis and became interested in both music and art early. He helped pay his way through art school by playing saxaphone in a jazz band on a Mississippi River boat. His first art work was for a small studio in St. Louis. After a few illustration assignments by mail, he decided to head for New York and quickly became the leader in a whole new school of illustration.

Humpty Dumpty
Cover for Life magazine, March 17, 1921

"The Comforts of Life Are Introduced Among the Indians"
Illustration for Knickerbocker's History of New York
by Washington Irving, 1899 edn.

Opposite Page

Collier's magazine cover, July 30, 1910

Maxfield Parrish (1870–1966)

ONE OF THE INTRIGUING QUESTIONS about Maxfield Parrish's work was how he obtained his beautiful translucent blue skies. He followed the Old Masters' practice of building up tones by means of glazes, one over another; this was a slow procedure, but Parrish preferred to work slowly. He even had his own machine shop for manufacturing the props and making models for his complex picture settings.

Parrish specialized in childhood fairy tales and mythology. His illustrated editions of Eugene Field's *Poems of Childhood,* Kenneth Grahame's *Dream Days,* and *The Knave of Hearts* by Louise Saunders have all become collectors' items, and his pictures were widely distributed as prints, which are also sought after. Among his major commissions were murals of "Old King Cole" for the old Knickerbocker Hotel in New York, "Sing a Song of Sixpence" for Hotel Sherman in Chicago, and several panels for offices of Curtis Publishing Co., in Philadelphia. Parrish continued to work even at an advanced age, and for years painted an annual landscape calendar for Brown & Bigelow.

Portrait drawing of Spencer Tracy
for WCBS-TV Award Theatre
Courtesy F. & M. Schaeffer Brewing Company

Fast Loose Money · Illustration for Cosmopolitan magazine, July, 1958

Opposite Page

Poster for the film "Camelot"
Reprinted courtesy of Warner Brothers,
Seven Arts, and Bill Gold Advertising, Inc

Robert Peak (born 1928)

ROBERT PEAK HAS BEEN ONE of the dominant illustrators of the past twenty years. At a time when the magazine market for illustration is declining steadily, he has found new outlets for his work. A typical example was his assignment to design a series of mural decorations for TWA to be reproduced on the reverse sides of the in-flight movie screens. This led to further projects for the airline, designing menu covers, guide books, covers for a quarterly magazine—altogether about fifty pieces of art over a three-year period. He has also designed posters for over fifty movies. Peak abandoned the customarily dismal montage of episodes from the film, and with outstanding interpretations—such as the design for *Camelot*—Peak has helped to raise the standards of movie poster art.

Over the years, Peak has continued to work for *Sports Illustrated* magazine (which has sent him on several reportorial assignments), *Time*, *T.V. Guide*, and for many national advertisers. Peak was elected to the Society of Illustrators Hall of Fame in 1977.

"The Magenta Village" from Holland Sketches,
Written and illustrated by Edward Penfield
Published by Charles Scribner's Sons, 1907

Edward Penfield (1866–1925)

At the turn of the century, there was a great deal of interest in the poster as a medium of art. Under the leadership of artists such as Toulouse-Lautrec, Alfons Mucha, and Théophile-Alexandre Steinlen in Europe, American illustrators produced many good examples of poster art. Edward Penfield was among the best of these illustrators.

Like all good poster artists, Penfield used strong, simple shapes that were clearly recognizable, even when viewed from a long distance. Yet within the shapes he included a sufficient amount of interesting detail to retain the viewer's interest close up. In addition to his posters, Penfield did a lot of cover illustrations for the magazines (which served the same purpose as posters) and calendar illustrations. He also wrote and illustrated an outstanding book, *Holland Sketches,* published by Scribner's in 1907. In addition to producing his own work, for a number of years Penfield acted as art director for *Harper's* magazine and teacher at the Art Students League.

Cover for Good Housekeeping magazine, March, 1914

Illustration for Holeproof Hosiery in the 1920s

Opposite Page

In a Position to Know
Cover illustration for Life magazine, April 7, 1921
Collection of J.B. Rund

Coles Phillips (1880–1927)

COLES PHILLIPS IS BEST REMEMBERED today for his special variation on the pretty-girl theme. This was his Fadeaway Girl. In an inventive series of differing images, a young woman's figure was displayed against a background that served to both camouflage and reveal her. Readers delighted in the device, and for many years the Fadeaway Girl appeared on covers of the old *Life* magazine and *Good Housekeeping*. Phillips is also remembered for his outstanding illustrations for Holeproof Hosiery—considered very daring in its day—and for Community Plate Silverware.

Phillips studied briefly at the Free School and the Chase School of Art in New York. After working briefly on staff in an art service, he opened his own agency. But he finally decided to devote himself solely to his art. He closed his agency, and allowed himself a month to break into the field. With the self-imposed deadline at hand and a single drawing under his arm, he approached the editor of *Life* and fortunately sold his first cover design. His career was launched and the Fadeaway Girl was born soon afterward.

116

Illustration for "Silver Knees," by Robert W. Chambers
Published in Liberty magazine, 1931

Drawing for "The Rake and the Hussy," by Robert W. Chambers
Published in Liberty magazine, 1929

Opposite Page

"Battle of Freeman's Farm" from Love and the Lieutenan
Reprinted from the Woman's Home Companion, 1931
Collection of Morris Weiss

Norman Price (1877–1951)

Norman Price was a Canadian, and he studied art in Toronto, London, and Paris. His first art work was done in London, and he was one of the founding partners of the Carlton Illustrators Studio there. When a branch of the studio was opened in New York, Norman was its representative; he moved permanently to the U.S. in 1911. He had already completed an important book illustration assignment, Lamb's *Tales from Shakespeare*, in England, and he began to do freelance illustration here, including a number of books, advertising campaigns, and magazine commissions. He particularly enjoyed historical subject matter and devoted so much research and care to rendering these pictures that art editors began to assign such stories to him exclusively. Among his best pictures were those done for stories by Robert W. Chambers. For many years, Price was active at the Society of Illustrators, establishing and adding to its library and archives of original illustrations. He was Honorary President from 1948 until his death and was elected to the Hall of Fame in 1978.

Illustration for The Story of King Arthur and His Knights,
Written and illustrated by Howard Pyle
Published by Charles Scribner's Sons, 1902

Illustration for The Ruby of Kishmoor,
Written and illustrated by Howard Pyle
Published by Harper and Brothers, 1908

Howard Pyle, N.A. (1853–1911)

THE TITLE, "FATHER OF AMERICAN ILLUSTRATION," may rightfully be given to Howard Pyle. Although he was certainly not the first, he came along early, and no one else has ever equaled the imaginative force of his pictures. He was also our greatest teacher of illustration. Through his classes at the Drexel Institute in Philadelphia and the Art Students League in New York, and finally his own classes at Chadds Ford, Pennsylvania, and Wilmington, Delaware, he inspired a whole generation of young artists, including Harvey Dunn, N.C. Wyeth, Frank Schoonover, and Jessie Willcox Smith.

Pyle was also a prolific author. He wrote *Men of Iron,* several volumes on the King Arthur legends, *The Merry Adventures of Robin Hood,* and other books and short stories.

Many of his pictures are in the permanent collection of the Delaware Art Museum; others are in the Brandywine Museum of Chadds Ford, established in the same old mill building that was the headquarters of the original Pyle summer school.

Illustration for Maxwell House Coffee, 1930

The Closing Door, 1922
Collection of Murray Tinkelman

Henry Raleigh (1880–1944)

For almost forty years Henry Raleigh was one of the most constant contributors to *The Saturday Evening Post*. His sophisticated renditions of high society made him a favorite with readers, and he illustrated stories by F. Scott Fitzgerald, William Faulkner, and most of the other prominent writers of his era. His drawings—a combination of drybrush and ink washes—look spontaneous and free; his sure touch was derived from his early years as a newspaper artist for the *San Francisco Examiner*.

It was William Randolph Hearst who recognized his talent and sent him to *The New York Journal*. In New York he illustrated magazine fiction for almost all major periodicals, in addition to illustrating for *The Saturday Evening Post* and advertising agencies. He is probably best remembered for his advertisements for Maxwell House Coffee.

Although Raleigh seldom exhibited; he was also a serious etcher and lithographer. Several of his original illustrations are in the Sanford Low Memorial Collection of American Illustration in the New Britain, Connecticut, Museum.

"Jumping on a Horse"
from "The Essentials at Fort Adobe"
Published in Harper's Monthly

"Captain Grimes' Battery Going up El Poso Hill" from "With the Fifth Corps"
Published in Harper's Monthly, November, 1898

Opposite Page

The Smoke Signal, 1905
Oil on canvas 38½ × 48¼"
Collection of the Amon Carter Museum
(Fort Worth, Texas)

Frederic Sackrider Remington, A.N.A. (1861–1909)

LIKE MANY YOUNG MEN of his era, Frederic Remington went west to seek his fortune. He had been a restless and undistinguished art student at Yale but was soon caught up in the excitement of the frontier West. He worked at various jobs from herding cattle to raising sheep, saw what was happening around him, and realized that the Old West was about to disappear. Remington now had a mission as an artist, to paint the Indians, cowboys, militia men, and settlers as they were, before civilization engulfed them. Remington sent some of his first drawings to *Harper's.* They were accepted but had to be redrawn by a staff artist for reproduction. Gradually, Remington's drawings improved, and eventually he joined the magazine staff. When the Spanish–American War came along, Remington was sent to Cuba with the troops as an artist-reporter. He became a friend of Theodore Roosevelt, and his painting of Roosevelt leading his Rough Riders in the charge on San Juan Hill helped to create the heroic image that later led to Roosevelt's election. Remington is best remembered for his fine paintings and bronzes.

From "Ambush on Camden Road," by John A. Leland
Collier's magazine, July 8, 1955

Opposite Page

The Donner Party
True magazine
Watercolor 24 × 44"
Collection Edward Cerullo

William Reusswig (1902–1978)

ONE OF THE MOST DRAMATIC AND TRAGIC STORIES of the westward migration was that of the Donner Party, which was trapped by weather in the Sierra Nevadas during the winter of 1846–47. Only half of the party survived the ordeal. In his painting of the subject, William Reusswig chose a panoramic view of the terrain, showing the long wagon train fighting through the heavy drifts and the backbreaking labor of trying to force the wagons up the steep inclines. Reusswig has specialized in reconstructing such historic episodes, and he was the author and illustrator of *A Picture Report of the Custer Fight*.

Reusswig was born in Sommerville, New Jersey, and attended Amherst College and the Art Students League in New York City. His illustration career began early with an assignment for *Collier's* magazine, and he contributed regularly thereafter to that publication as well as to *Redbook, True,* and many other magazines.

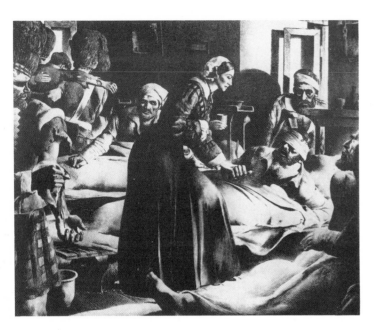

Florence Nightingale
Advertising illustration for Parke Davis, 1937

Dust Bowl
Advertising illustration for Purolator
© 1941 Purolator Products

Opposite Page

Boris Godunov
For the Capehart Corp., 1945
Opaque watercolor

Robert Riggs, N.A. (1896–1970)

The subjects of Riggs's pictures always seem larger than life, and his compositions are similarly dramatic and powerful. As a lithographer, Riggs learned to exploit fully the effect of the black and white of the stone, and he translated this same impact into his editorial and advertising illustrations.

Riggs studied at the Art Students League in New York for a year before serving in the army during World War I. After the armistice he stayed in Paris for further study at the Académie Julien. When he returned to America, he found a job as a sketch artist for the N.W. Ayer Advertising Agency. Gradually, he began to do the finished art and his illustrations became consistent award winners. Meanwhile, he continued to work in lithography and to exhibit his prints. These are now in many private collections and museums, including the Brooklyn Museum and the Library of Congress.

A Perfect Death · Life magazine, Dec. 22, 1958 © 1958 Time, Inc.

Morton Roberts (1927–1964)

MORTON ROBERTS WAS BORN IN WORCESTER, Massachusetts, and graduated from the Yale University School of Fine Arts. He successfully competed for the Edwin Austin Abbey Fellowship from the National Academy of Design and regularly contributed to the Academy shows and to the American Watercolor Society.

His illustration career was spectacular but short and could surely have been a great one had he lived longer. He illustrated for the major magazines, beginning with *Collier's,* but his outstanding assignments were for *Life* magazine. In his work for *Life* he provided a picture counterpart for several special features, such as the story of jazz, and "Russia and the Revolution," in which he gave dramatic excitement to the subjects in paintings that combined a modern and an academic approach.

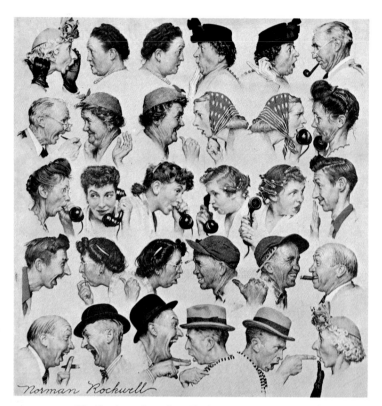

The Coward
Life magazine cover, April 10,

Norman Rockwell (1894–1979)

NORMAN ROCKWELL HAD THE COMMON TOUCH; his pictures were recognized and loved by millions of Americans. His painting skill was immense and transcended a literal photographic rendition of his subjects. He believed intensely in old-fashioned virtures and in homespun characters; it is the warmth of that belief that comes across so clearly.

Rockwell never graduated from high school. He attended art classes at the National Academy of Design and at the Art Students League and began illustrating for *Boy's Life* magazine while still in his teens. By twenty-one, he had sold his first cover to *The Saturday Evening Post* and eventually produced over three hundred more.

During World War II, Rockwell did his bit through his famous paintings illustrating the "Four Freedoms." After the war he turned to stronger themes, such as integration, the Peace Corps, and the Golden Rule. He painted portraits of presidents Kennedy, Johnson, Eisenhower, and Nixon, and world leaders including Nehru of India and Nasser of Egypt. He has been the subject of books and honors, and was elected to the Hall of Fame.

Postage stamp based on "Jerked Down," 1964, commemorating 100th year of artist's birth

When Law Dulls the Edge of Chance

Opposite Page

Jerked Down, 1907
Oil on canvas 22½ × 36½"
Collection, Thomas Gilcrease Institute
of American History and Art

Charles Marion Russell (1864–1926)

CHARLES RUSSELL AND Frederic Remington are preeminent among Western artists. They were almost the same age and painted similar subject matter, but their paths apparently never crossed. Remington had the advantage of an art education, and his career was off to an earlier start. Russell was self-taught, and it took him a long time before his art skills caught up with his knowledge of the West.

In his youth he worked with a fur trapper, wrangled horses, and lived with the Blackfoot Indians for months at a time. Remington often depicted troopers in battle against the Indians in his pictures, while Russell was the more tolerant and made many paintings sympathetic to the Indian. Like Remington, Russell also made many excellent bronzes; his sculptures of animals are particularly perceptive.

One of his finest works is the mural entitled *Lewis and Clark Meeting the Flathead Indians at Ross' Hole,* for the capitol building of Montana. Russell's studio was in Montana, and two museum collections of his work are in the state: the Trigg-Russell Gallery at Great Falls and the Historical Society of Montana in Helena.

Cover from The Saturday Evening Post
Copyright © 1942 by the Curtis Publishing Company

Opposite Page

Highwayman
Oil on canvas 30 × 45"
Collection of the New York Society of Illustrators

Mead Schaeffer (born 1898)

As a student of Harvey Dunn and Dean Cornwell, Schaeffer learned to paint in the Howard Pyle tradition, and he often dealt with similar subject matter. Over the years, he completed a series of sixteen illustrated classics for Dodd Mead and Company including such titles as *Moby Dick, Typee, Les Misérables, The Count of Monte Cristo,* and *Tom Cringle's Log.* He was also a regular contributor to most of the magazines.

When *The Saturday Evening Post* began to feature cover subjects dealing with regional Americana, Schaeffer became a regular contributor. This required a considerable amount of travel across the country looking for ideas (he made one trip west with his friend, Norman Rockwell). This travel resulted in cover subjects ranging from drilling for oil to collecting sap for maple syrup. During World War II, Schaeffer's covers featured representative members of the various armed services. These were done with the cooperation and assistance of United States military authorities.

"Runaway Horses," illustration for Cinders
Published in American Magazine, November, 1914

Illustration for "Rustlers of Silver River," by Zane Grey
Published in The Country Gentleman, December, 1929

Opposite Page

Illustration for "The Test," by Rex Beach
Published by McClure's magazine, December, 1904
Collection of the author

Frank Schoonover (1877–1972)

FRANK SCHOONOVER WAS ONE OF the select inner circle of Howard Pyle students who served as teaching assistants. He took over the studios after Pyle's death in 1911 and continued to teach and work in the studios for the rest of his long life.

At Pyle's suggestion, Schoonover made an extended trip to the Hudson Bay region as background research for manuscript assignments he had received. This trip and another one later served to make him an expert on the Indian life of the area. When he wrote and illustrated his book, *Lafitte, the Pirate of the Gulf,* he also prepared for it with an extended visit to the Mississippi Bayou. Schoonover was the illustrator for Jack London's *White Fang,* the orginal *Hopalong Cassidy* story by Clarence Mulford and *Cardigan* by Robert W. Chambers. He was a regular contributor to *Country Gentleman, American Boy, Boy's Life, Red Book,* and many other magazines. His illustrations and paintings are to be found in many collections, including the Glenbow–Alberta Institute of Calgary, the Delaware Art Museum, and the Brandywine Museum in Chadd's Ford, Pa.

From "Crazy Waters," by Leonard H. Nason
The Saturday Evening Post © 1938 Curtis Publ. Co.
Charcoal and blue washes 29½ × 23"

From "Valedictory,"
by MacKinlay Kantor
Pen and Ink
Published by
Coward-McCann, Inc

Amos Sewell (born 1901)

Amos Sewell supported himself as a bank teller by day while he attended night classes at the California School of Fine Arts. Wanting to be an illustrator, he headed east by way of the Panama Canal as a working deck hand on a lumber boat. He studied with Guy Pène DuBois and Julian Levi at the Art Students League and with Harvey Dunn at the Grand Central Art School.

At the same time, he began to obtain assignments for black-and-white pulp illustrations and soon became one of the best in the field. Later he obtained his first manuscript for the slicks from *Country Gentleman* and soon added other magazine clients, including the prestigious *Saturday Evening Post*, with which he formed a long association. Sewell depicted children particularly well, and he illustrated a series of short stories by R. Ross Annett that continued for over twenty years. He also painted many *Post* covers, most of which featured youngsters.

Illustration for "The White Invader," by James Warner Bellah
Published in The Saturday Evening Post
Copyright © 1950 by the Curtis Publishing Company

Book illustration from Death Comes for the Archbishop, by Willa Cather
Copyright © 1929–1933 by Alfred A. Knopf, Inc.

Harold Von Schmidt (born 1893)

HAROLD VON SCHMIDT WAS BORN in California and was brought up by his grandfather—a forty-niner. As a young man, a series of rough-and-tumble jobs gave him a tough discipline that later helped him as an illustrator of adventure and western stories.

His first art training was at the San Francisco Art Institute and the California College of Arts and Crafts. Among his teachers were Worth Ryder and Maynard Dixon. After some illustration experience with *Sunset* magazine and a job as a poster artist with Foster & Kleiser, a billboard firm, Von Schmidt won a national poster contest and decided to go east to try to get illustration work. He also enrolled in the classes conducted by Harvey Dunn. Dunn did not teach how to paint but how to think about picture making, and Von Schmidt learned to differentiate between incident and epic in illustration. He has since illustrated for virtually all magazines and is best known for his Western paintings.

Von Schmidt served as president of the Society of Illustrators in 1938–41 and has been elected into the Society's Hall of Fame. He also received the first gold medal from the National Cowboy Hall of Fame in 1968.

Frontispiece, Rhymes of Real Children, by Betty Sage
Published by Fox, Duffield, and Company, 1903

Advertising illustration for Ivory Soap, 1902

Opposite Page

Illustration for A Child's Garden of Verses,
by Robert Louis Stevenson
Published by Charles Scribner's Sons, 1905

Jessie Willcox Smith (1863–1935)

J ESSIE WILLCOX SMITH FIRST planned to be a kindergarten teacher, and she was interested in children all her life. However, it was the instruction she received at the Drexel Institute under Howard Pyle that made it possible for her to combine her love of art and children, and she became one of America's foremost illustrators.

She was called upon by many of the magazines to illustrate stories involving mothers and babies, young children and child psychology. For *Good Housekeeping* magazine alone, she did almost two hundred cover designs. Jessie Smith illustrated many books as well, including special editions of classics, such as: *Heidi, Little Women,* Robert Louis Stevenson's *A Child's Garden of Verses,* and *A Book of Old Stories.*

She did many appealing Ivory Soap illustrations for Procter and Gamble. Jessie Smith was a member of the Philadelphia Watercolor Club, Fellowship of the Pennsylvania Academy of Fine Arts, and the New York Watercolor Club. She won numerous awards including a Silver Medal at the Panama–Pacific Exposition in San Francisco in 1915.

From "The Miracle Goat," by Kay Boyle
Woman's Home Companion, Jan., 1947

From "Commodore Hornblower," by C.S. Forester
The Saturday Evening Post
Copyright© 1945 Curtis Publ. Co.

Opposite Page

From McCall's magazine

Ben Stahl (born 1910)

Much of Ben Stahl's art education came from boyhood visits with his grandmother to the Chicago Art Institute and the Marshall Field Art Galleries. His first job was errand boy and mat cutter in a Chicago art studio. With this entrée into the world of commercial art, he watched over the shoulders of the staff illustrators and soaked up everything he could learn. Within five years he was a full-fledged illustrator himself with one of the top studios. One of his pictures attracted the attention of *The Saturday Evening Post,* and he was given his first magazine story to illustrate. This led to many other illustrations for the *Post* and for most of the other magazines.

Stahl always drew on the inspiration of his early museum visits; he was particularly impressed by Degas. This impressionist influence became more pronounced in his work and found enthusiastic response from art editors and the public.

Hitch Four Widows to the Plow
Advertising illustration for Lysol Disinfectant, 1931

Opposite Page

The Baker's Dozen
Advertising illustration for
The Gilbert Paper Company, 1942

Saul Tepper (born 1899)

SAUL TEPPER HAS PURSUED CAREERS IN BOTH ART AND MUSIC. Art came first. Tepper won a correspondence-course art contest when he was a youngster and continued his studies at Cooper Union, the Art Students League, and with Harvey Dunn at the Grand Central School of Art. To make a living, Tepper worked as a letterer for a fashion art studio and eventually graduated to making product illustrations for advertisers and then story illustrations for the magazines. During his illustration career, he divided his time about equally between editorial and advertising work. As a writer of popular songs, he is also a member of ASCAP and AGAC. His compositions have been recorded by stars such as Ella Fitzgerald, Ezio Pinza, Glenn Miller, Nat (King) Cole, and Harry James. Tepper also wrote sketches, music, and lyrics for the annual shows of the Society of Illustrators.

From "Litton Shoots for the Moon,"
by William B. Harris
Fortune magazine, April, 1958

The Seventh Generation
Cosmopolitan magazine

Opposite Page

Construction Workers
Acrylic on board 20 × 24"
Collection the author

Robert Weaver (born 1924)

Rᴏʙᴇʀᴛ Wᴇᴀᴠᴇʀ ʜᴀs ʜᴇʟᴘᴇᴅ ᴛᴏ ᴄʜᴀɴɢᴇ ᴛʜᴇ ғᴜɴᴄᴛɪᴏɴ of the illustrator. He believes that there should be a more active participation of the illustrator in the planning stage and prefers to sit in on such sessions with advertisers or editors. This, in fact, has become a more common practice, and less editorial constraint has allowed the artist to make more personal statements about the subjects depicted. This has also provided a climate for creativity that has helped to narrow the gap between "commercial" and "fine" art.

Weaver is from Pittsburgh, and he studied art at the Carnegie-Mellon Institute there, followed by classes at the Art Students League in New York and the Academia Delle Belle Arti in Venice. His clients have included *Fortune* magazine, *Life, Sports Illustrated, Town and Country, Esquire, True, Seventeen,* and many other magazines.

Illustration for "Sayonara," by James E. Michener
Published in McCall's magazine, October, 1953

Collier's cover, December 23, 1939

Opposite Page

Illustration for "Your Ideal Girl," by Eileen Herbert Jordan
Reprinted from Good Housekeeping, August, 1953
Collection of the artist

Jon Whitcomb (born 1906)

JON WHITCOMB ORIGINALLY PLANNED to be a writer and, in fact, graduated from Ohio State University as a writing major. Midway through school, however, he landed a summer job painting posters for a Cleveland movie theater and became so good at it that following graduation he was transferred to Chicago to work for a large theater chain. From there, he returned to an art service in Cleveland where he did a variety of commercial art and illustration; next he went to the New York branch of the studio where the clients were even more diversified. It was an excellent training ground for an illustrator, and *Collier's* gave Whitcomb his first story. It was very well received and other magazines soon followed. Whitcomb's busy career was interrupted by World War II when he served three years as a lieutenant, j.g. in the navy. Part of the time he painted morale-building pictures, but he was also a combat artist in the invasions of Tinian, Guam, and Peleliu. His career resumed after the war, and he also made use of his writing skills by contributing a monthly feature for *Cosmopolitan* magazine in which he illustrated and wrote about the theatrical and movie world. Whitcomb has written two children's books about poodles and a book about glamor girls, *All About Girls*.

Illustration for "A World Apart," by Mel Heimer
Published in McCall's magazine, November, 1963

Illustration for "The Visitor," by Audrey A. Boughton
Published in The Saturday Evening Post
Copyright © 1965 by the Curtis Publishing Company

Coby Whitmore (born 1913)

As a specialist in illustrating love stories for *McCall's, Ladies' Home Journal, Redbook, Good Housekeeping, Cosmopolitan,* and other magazines, Coby Whitmore had the endless problem of making each picture look different. Although the logical highlight of a majority of the manuscripts involved "the clinch"—and variations on this theme would seem to be limited—Whitmore was always able to come up with something new. Another requirement was a thorough knowledge of fashion trends. Since the pictures oftentimes were not published until several months after being painted, styles chosen had to be advanced enough to avoid looking dated when they appeared.

Whitmore is from Ohio and attended the Dayton Art Institute. He was then apprenticed to the Sundblom–Henry Art Studio in Chicago where he learned the professional rudiments of commercial art. After some other interim studio jobs, he moved to New York and a long association with the Charles E. Cooper studio. From this base he began to illustrate for the major magazines.

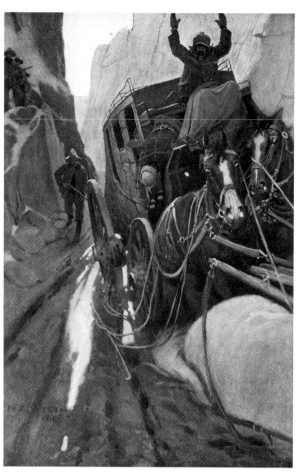

"Hands Up" from
"The Story of Montana,"
by C.P. Connolly
Published in McClure's magazine
Collection of Walter Reed Bimson
Valley National Bank, Phoenix

Moose Hunters
From Scribner's magazine

Opposite Page

The Hunter · Illustration for "The Indian in His Solitude"
Published in Outing magazine, June, 1907
Collection of the Brandywine Museum

Newell Convers Wyeth, N.A. (1882–1945)

Like most illustrators, N. C. Wyeth took his art very seriously. In addition to a heavy schedule of picture assignments, he always took the time to paint still lifes, landscapes, portraits, and other subjects for exhibition. He produced an illustrious group of children: Andrew, now even more famous than his father; Henriette and Caroline, who are both accomplished painters; and Ann, a composer. Grandson Jamie is also carrying on the family painting tradition.

Wyeth was one of Howard Pyle's star pupils. While still under Pyle's instruction, he began to obtain his first illustration assignments and quickly developed his own highly dramatic point of view. This approach was especially appropriate for the long series of Charles Scribner's Sons Classics he illustrated, such as Robert Louis Stevenson's *Kidnapped* and *Treasure Island,* James Fennimore Cooper's *Last of the Mohicans,* and Jules Verne's *Mysterious Island.* In addition to the more than twenty-five titles in this series, he illustrated many other books, worked for most of the major magazines (his illustrations probably totaled as many as 3000), and did many major mural commissions.

From "Alice of Old Vincennes"
Published by Bowen-Merrill Co., 1900

From "Engine No. 8," by Caroline Duer
Scribner's magazine, August, 1902

Opposite Page

From "The Story of the Revolution,"
By Henry Cabot Lodge
Published by Charles Scribner's Sons, 1898
Oil on canvas 36 × 27"

Frederick Coffay Yohn (1875–1933)

ALTHOUGH FREDERICK YOHN ILLUSTRATED A WIDE VARIETY of subject matter during his long career, he is best remembered for his documentation of wars and battle, beginning with the Spanish–American War in 1898. He also did many paintings recreating earlier historical episodes. Among them were his outstanding illustrations for *The Story of the Revolution* by Henry Cabot Lodge, General Funstan's *Memoirs of Two Wars,* and a deluxe edition of Bulwer-Lytton's *Last Days of Pompeii.*

Yohn was from Indianapolis and attended the Indianapolis Art School as well as the Art Students League in New York, where he studied under H. Siddons Mowbray. He made his debut as an illustrator at nineteen and for many years illustrated regularly for *Harper's* and *Scribner's* and many other prominent magazines. In 1930 Yohn was commissioned to paint several historical canvases for the Massachusetts Bay Tercentenary.